SUPER EASY SONGBOOK

JOHNNY CASH

ISBN 978-1-5400-4314-6

Visit Hal Leonard Online at
www.halleonard.com

Contact us:
Hal Leonard
7777 West Bluemound Road
Milwaukee, WI 53213
Email: info@halleonard.com

In Europe, contact:
Hal Leonard Europe Limited
42 Wigmore Street
Marylebone, London, W1U 2RN
Email: info@halleonardeurope.com

In Australia, contact:
Hal Leonard Australia Pty. Ltd.
4 Lentara Court
Cheltenham, Victoria, 3192 Australia
Email: info@halleonard.com.au

Welcome to the *Super Easy Songbook* series!

This unique collection will help you play your favorite songs quickly and easily. Here's how it works:

- Play the simplified melody with your right hand. Letter names appear inside each note to assist you.

- There are no key signatures to worry about! If a sharp ♯ or flat ♭ is needed, it is shown beside the note each time.

- There are no page turns, so your hands never have to leave the keyboard.

- If two notes are connected by a tie ⌣, hold the first note for the combined number of beats. (The second note does not show a letter name since it is not re-struck.)

- Add basic chords with your left hand using the provided keyboard diagrams. Chord voicings have been carefully chosen to minimize hand movement.

- The left-hand rhythm is up to you, and chord notes can be played together or separately. Be creative!

- If the chords sound muddy, move your left hand an octave* higher. If this gets in the way of playing the melody, move your right hand an octave higher as well.

  An octave spans eight notes. If your starting note is C, the next C to the right is an octave higher.

———————————— ALSO AVAILABLE ————————————

Hal Leonard Student Keyboard Guide HL00296039

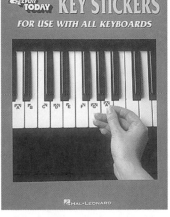

Key Stickers HL00100016

All Over Again

Words and Music by
John R. Cash

Moderately bright

Ev - 'ry time I look at you, I fall in love

all o - ver a - gain. Ev - 'ry

time I think of you, it all be - gins

all o - ver a - gain.

One lit - tle dream at night and I can dream all day. It

Big River

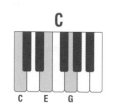
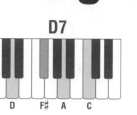
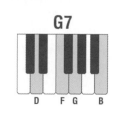
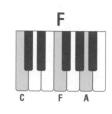

Words and Music by
Johnny Cash

Now, I taught the weep - ing wil - low how to cry. _____

_____ And I showed the clouds how to cov - er up a

clear blue sky. And the tears that I cried for that

wom - an are gon - na flood you, Big Riv - er. Then

I'm gon - na sit right here un - til I die. _____

Don't Take Your Guns to Town

Words and Music by
Johnny R. Cash

A young cow-boy named Bil-ly Joe grew rest-less on the farm. A
boy filled with wan-der-lust, who real-ly meant no harm. He
changed his clothes and shined his boots and combed his dark hair down, and his
moth-er cried as he walked out, "Don't take your guns to town, son.
Leave your guns at home, Bill. Don't take your guns to town."

Cry, Cry, Cry

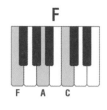 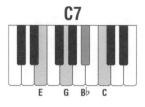 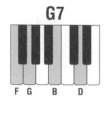 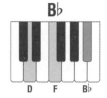

Words and Music by
Johnny Cash

Moderately bright

Ev - 'ry - bod - y   knows   where   you   go   when   the
Soon   your   sug - ar   dad - dies   will

sun   goes   down.   I   think   you   on - ly
all   be   gone.   You'll   wake   up   some

live   to   see   the   lights   up - town.   I
cold   day   and   find   you're   a - lone.   You'll

wast - ed   my   time   when   I   would   try,   try,
call   for   me,   but   I'm   gon - na   tell   you   bye,   bye,

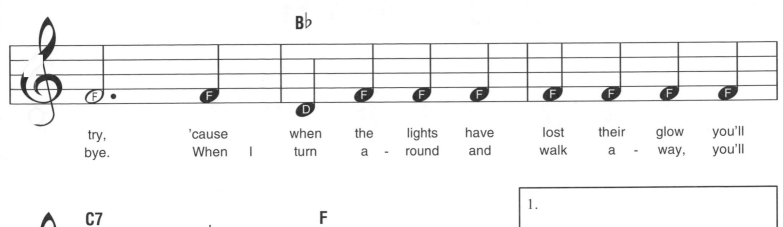

Bb

try,
bye.

'cause when the lights have lost their glow you'll
When I when turn a - round and walk a - way, you'll

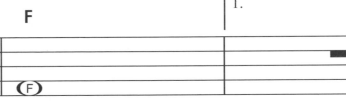

C7   **F**   1.

cry,   cry,   cry.
cry,   cry,   cry.

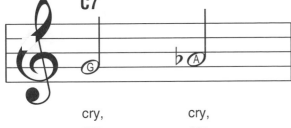

2.

You're gon - na cry, cry, cry, and you'll

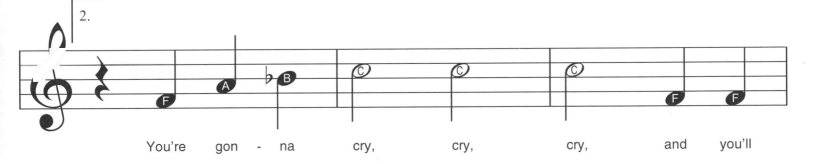

Bb   **F**   **Bb**

cry   a - lone.   When   ev - 'ry - one's   for -

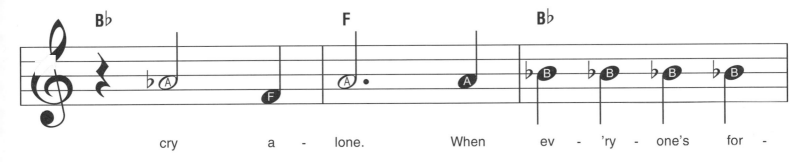

F

got - ten   and   you're   left   on   your   own,   you're   gon - na

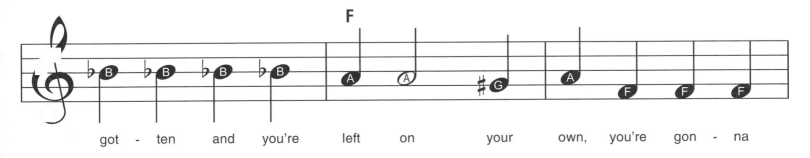

G7   **C7**   **F**

cry,   cry,   cry. _____

Daddy Sang Bass

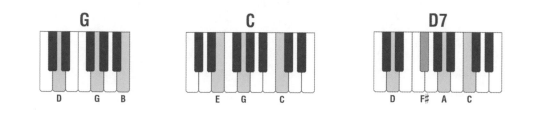

Words and Music by
Carl Perkins

Moderately bright

Dad-dy sang bass, Ma-ma sang ten-or, me and lit-tle broth-er would join right in there. Sing-in' seems to help a trou-bled soul. One of these days, and it won't be long, I'll re-join them in a

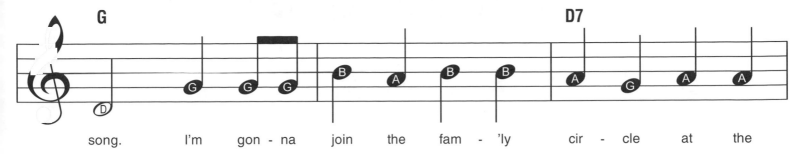

song. I'm gon - na join the fam - 'ly cir - cle at the

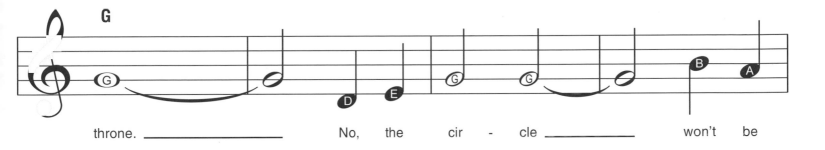

throne. _____ No, the cir - cle _____ won't be

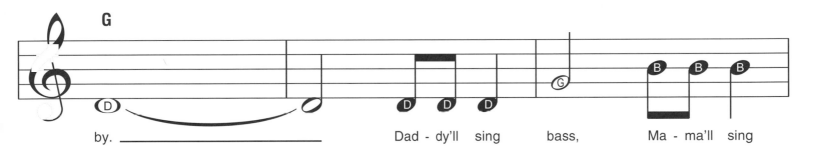

bro - ken _____ by and by, Lord, by and

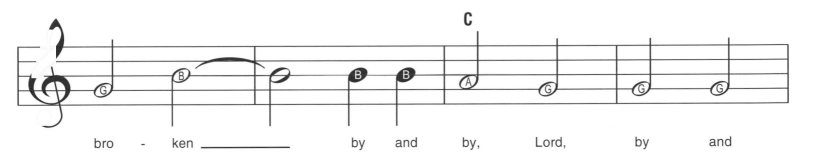

by. _____ Dad - dy'll sing bass, Ma - ma'll sing

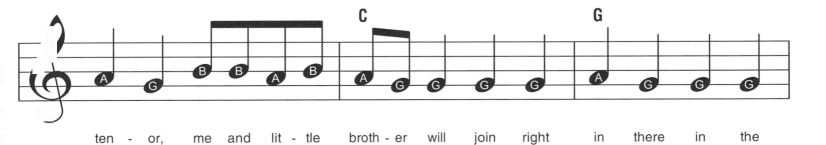

ten - or, me and lit - tle broth - er will join right in there in the

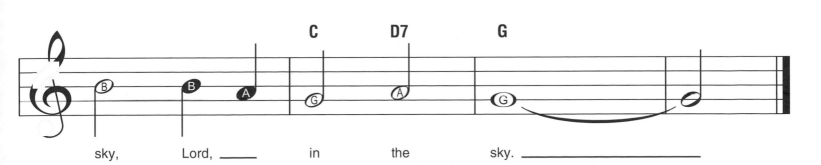

sky, Lord, ____ in the sky. _____

Flesh and Blood

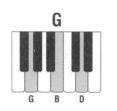
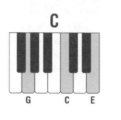
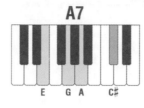
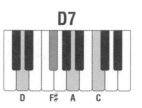

Words and Music by
Johnny Cash

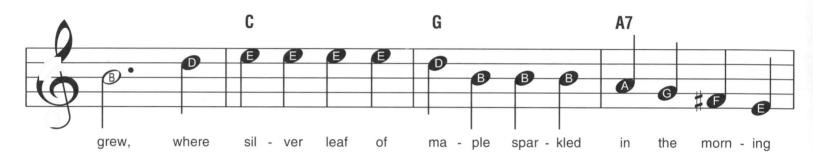

Be - side a sing - in' moun - tain stream where the pus - sy wil - low

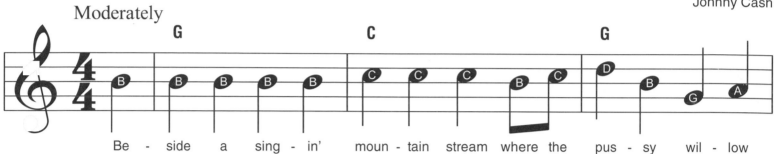

grew, where sil - ver leaf of ma - ple spar - kled in the morn - ing

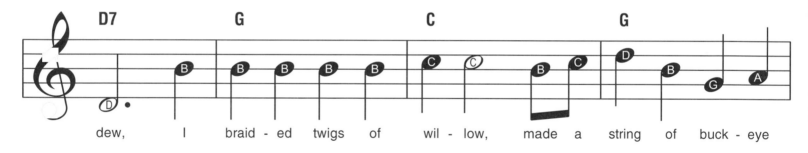

dew, I braid - ed twigs of wil - low, made a string of buck - eye

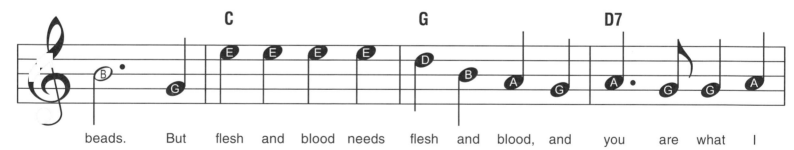

beads. But flesh and blood needs flesh and blood, and you are what I

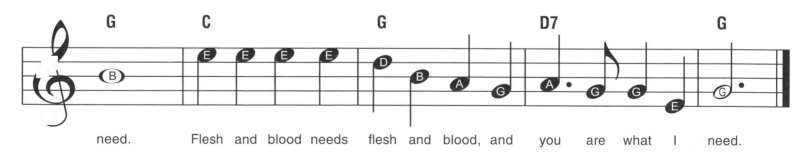

need. Flesh and blood needs flesh and blood, and you are what I need.

Hey, Porter

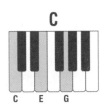
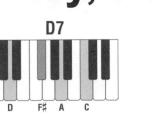
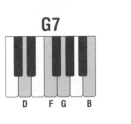
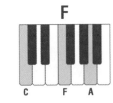

Words and Music by
John R. Cash

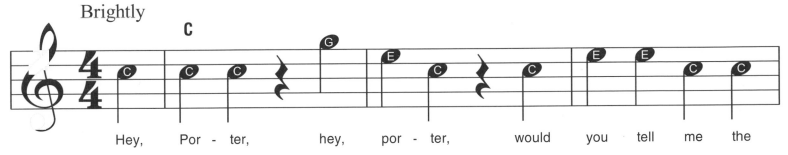

Hey, Por - ter, hey, por - ter, would you tell me the

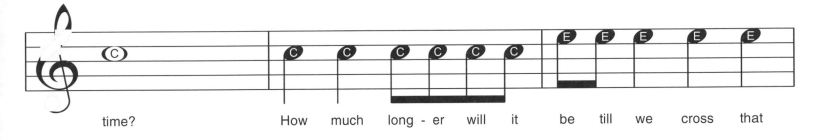

time? How much long - er will it be till we cross that

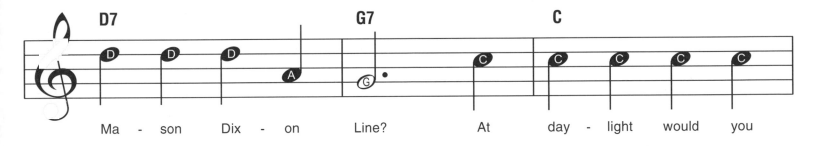

Ma - son Dix - on Line? At day - light would you

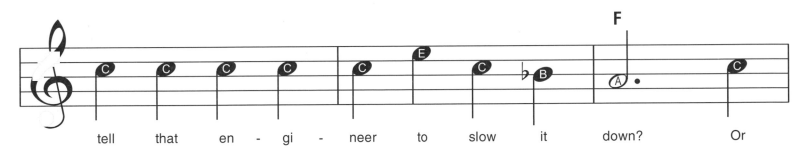

tell that en - gi - neer to slow it down? Or

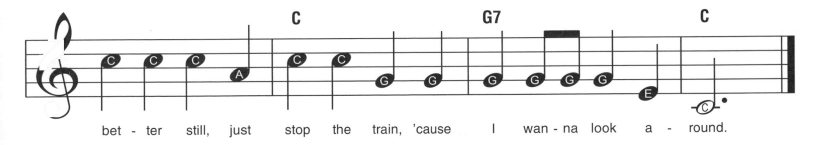

bet - ter still, just stop the train, 'cause I wan - na look a - round.

Folsom Prison Blues

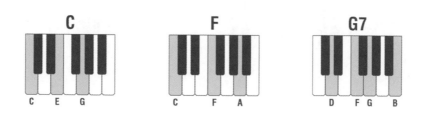

Words and Music by
John R. Cash

Moderately

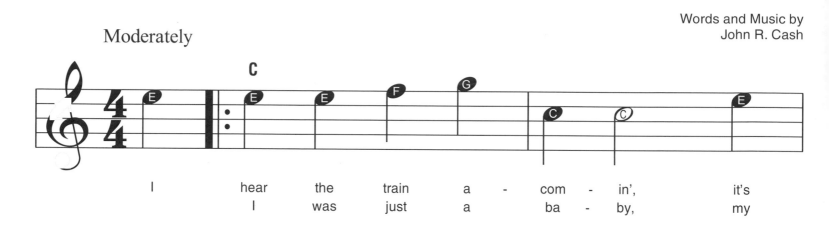

I   hear   the   train   a -   com -   in',   it's
I   was   just   a   ba -   by,   my

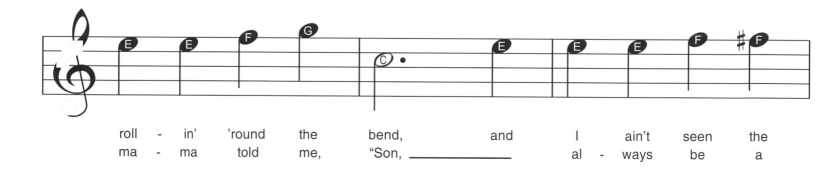

roll - in'   'round   the   bend,   and   I   ain't   seen   the
ma - ma   told   me,   "Son, _____   al - ways   be   a

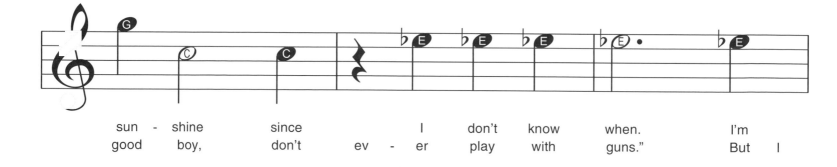

sun - shine   since   I   don't   know   when.   I'm
good   boy,   don't   ev - er   play   with   guns."   But   I

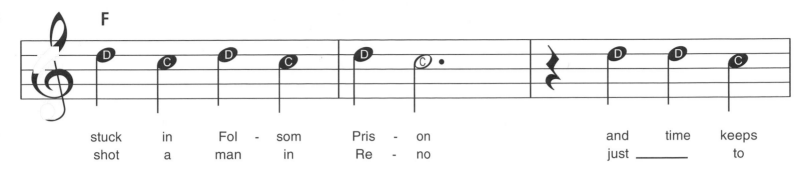

stuck   in   Fol - som   Pris - on   and   time   keeps
shot   a   man   in   Re - no   just ____ to

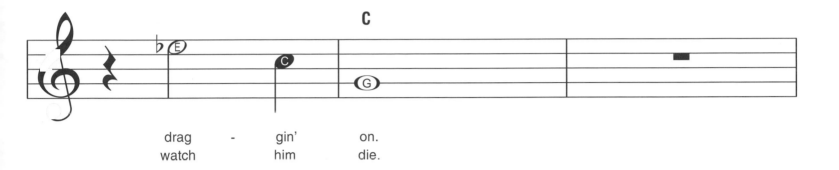

drag - gin'   on.
watch   him   die.

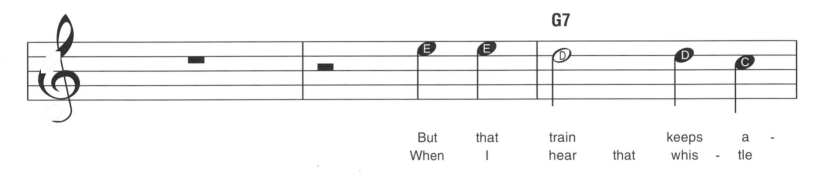

But   that   train   keeps   a -
When   I   hear   that   whis - tle

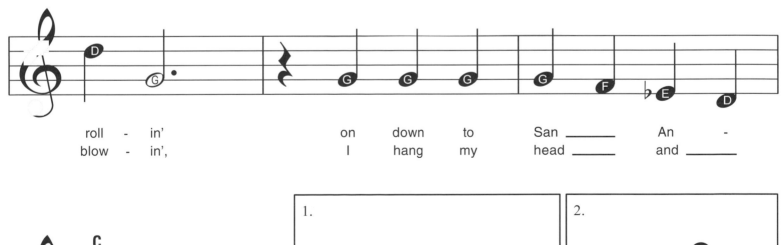

roll - in'   on   down   to   San ____ An -
blow - in',   I   hang   my   head ____ and ____

tone.   When
cry.

(Ghost) Riders in the Sky
(A Cowboy Legend)
from RIDERS IN THE SKY

By Stan Jones

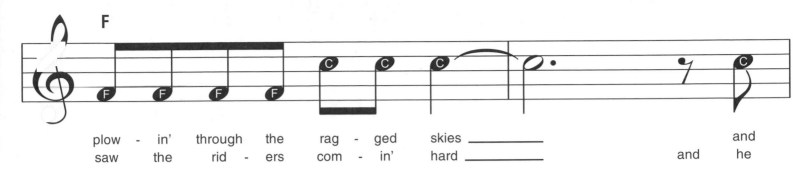

plow - in' through the rag - ged skies _____ and
saw the rid - ers com - in' hard _____ and he

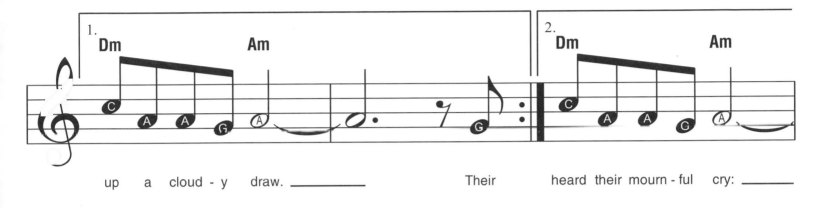

up a cloud - y draw. _____ Their

heard their mourn - ful cry: _____

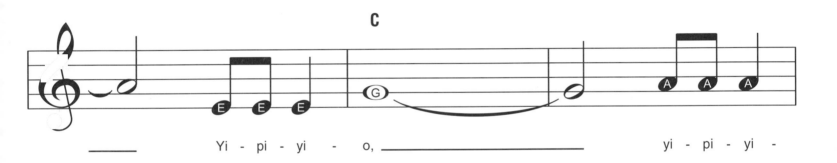

_____ Yi - pi - yi - o, _____ yi - pi - yi -

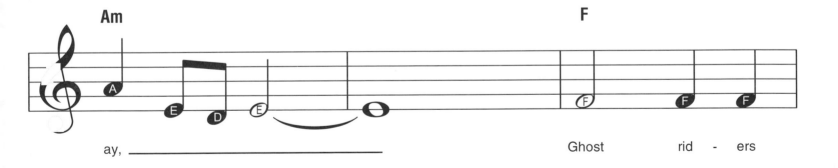

ay, _____ Ghost rid - ers

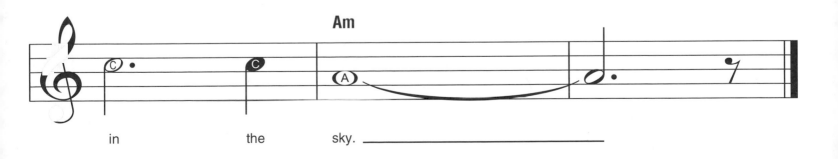

in the sky. _____

Guess Things Happen That Way

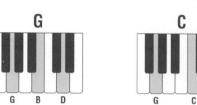  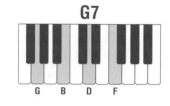

Words and Music by
Jack Clement

Moderately bright

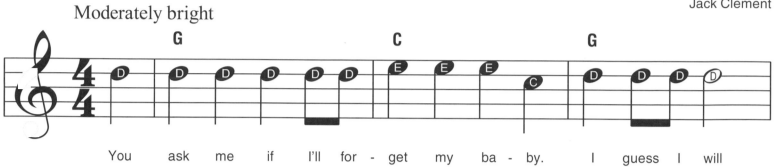

You ask me if I'll for-get my ba-by. I guess I will

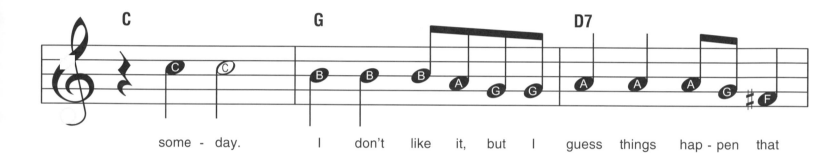

some-day. I don't like it, but I guess things hap-pen that

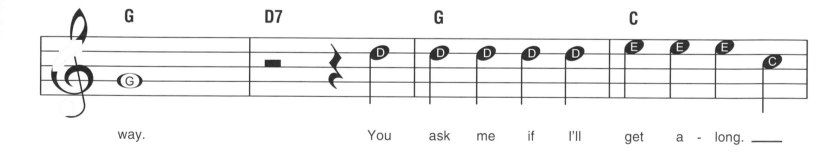

way. You ask me if I'll get a-long. ____

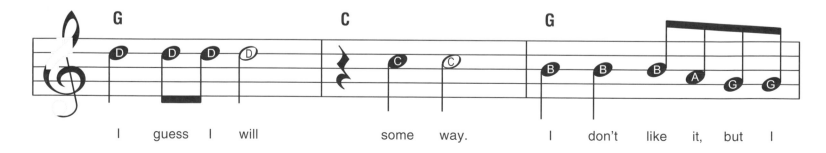

I guess I will some way. I don't like it, but I

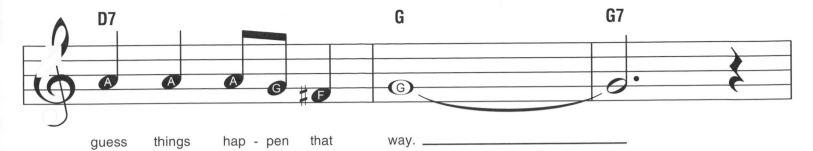

guess things hap - pen that way. _____

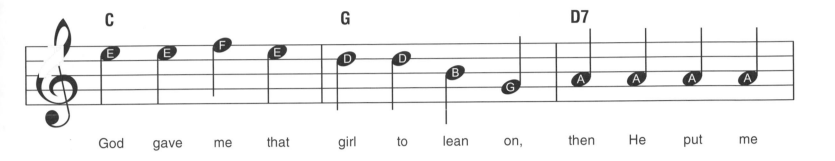

God gave me that girl to lean on, then He put me

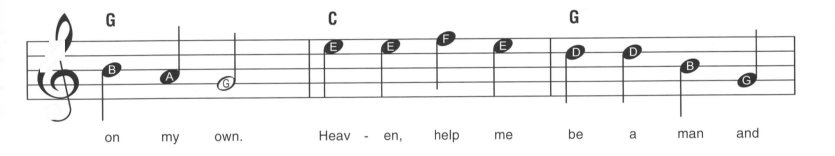

on my own. Heav - en, help me be a man and

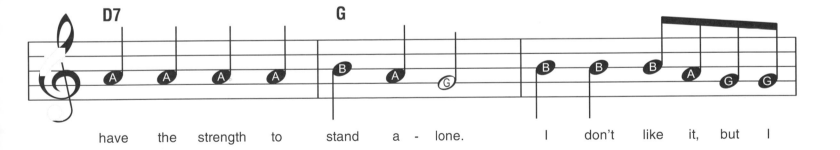

have the strength to stand a - lone. I don't like it, but I

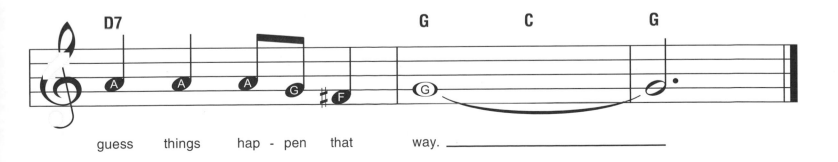

guess things hap - pen that way. _____

I Walk the Line

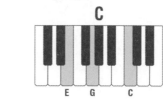
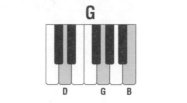
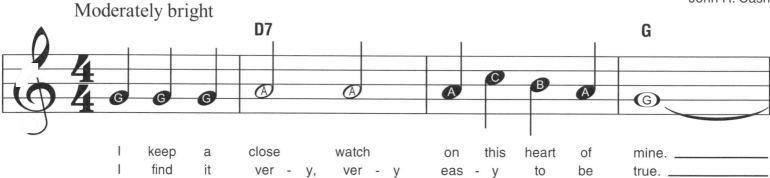

Words and Music by
John R. Cash

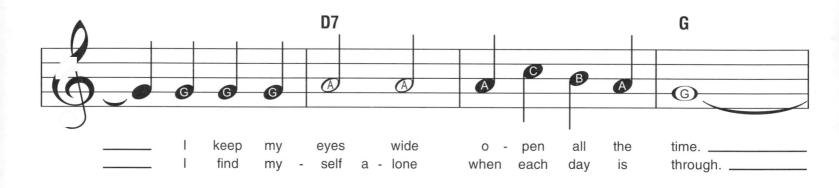

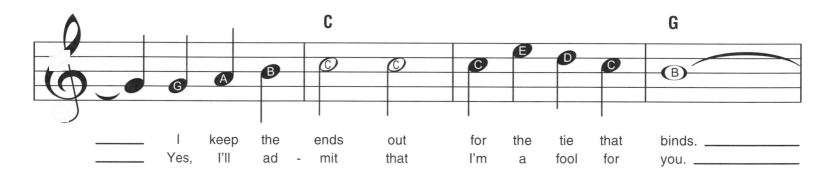

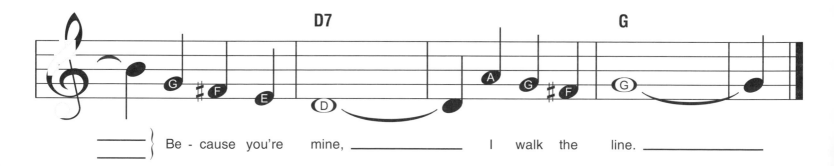

I've Been Everywhere

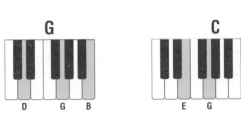 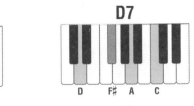

Words and Music by
Geoff Mack

If I Were a Carpenter

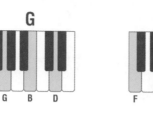
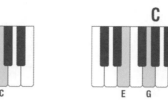

Words and Music by
Tim Hardin

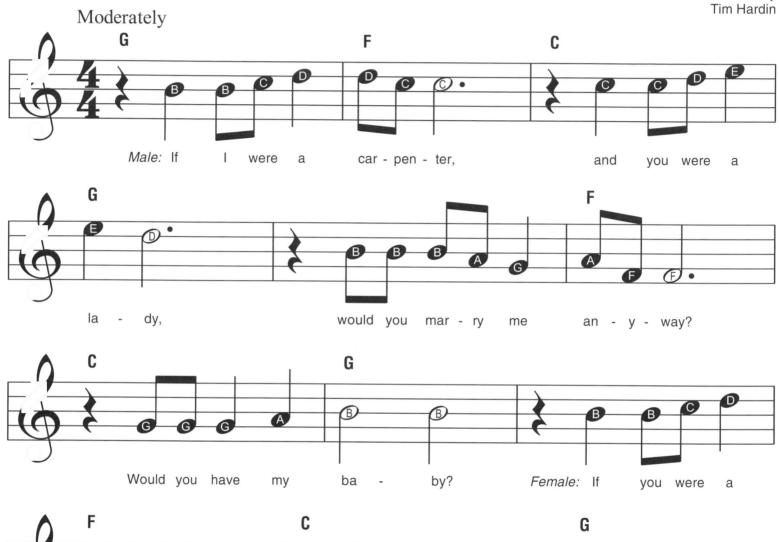

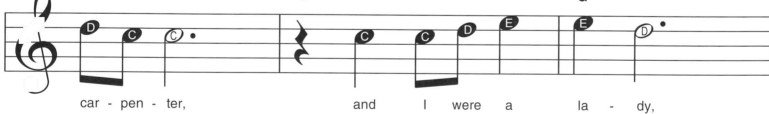

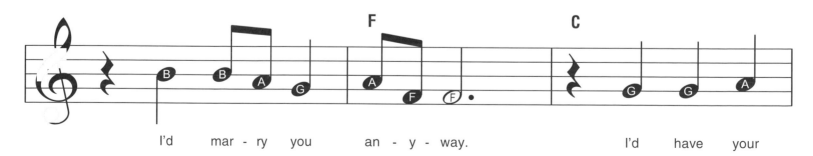

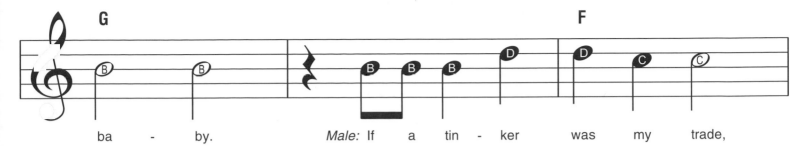

ba - by. *Male:* If a tin - ker was my trade,

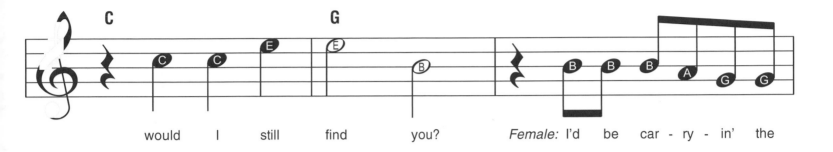

would I still find you? *Female:* I'd be car - ry - in' the

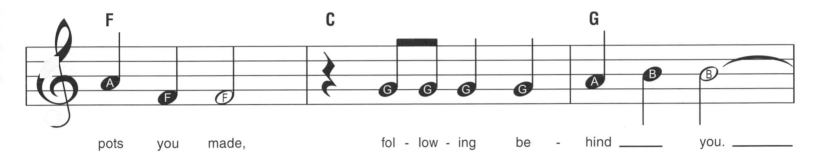

pots you made, fol - low - ing be - hind _____ you. _____

_____ *Both:* Save your love through lone - li - ness,

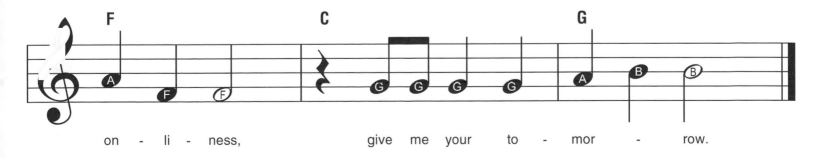

save your love through sor - row. I gave you my

on - li - ness, give me your to - mor - row.

The Man in Black

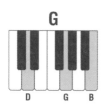
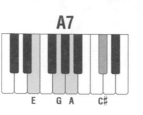
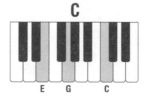
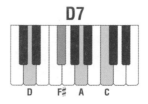

Words and Music by
John R. Cash

Moderately

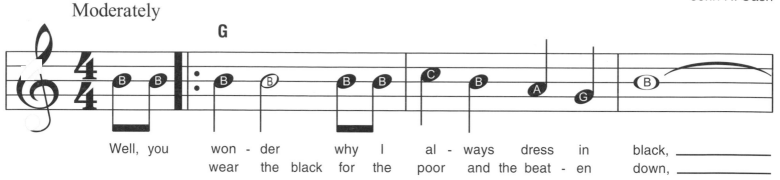

Well, you won - der why I al - ways dress in black, _____
wear the black for the poor and the beat - en down, _____

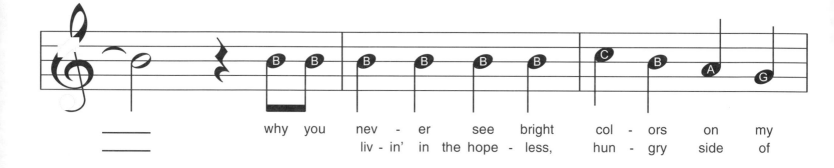

_____ why you nev - er see bright col - ors on my
_____ liv - in' in the hope - less, hun - gry side of

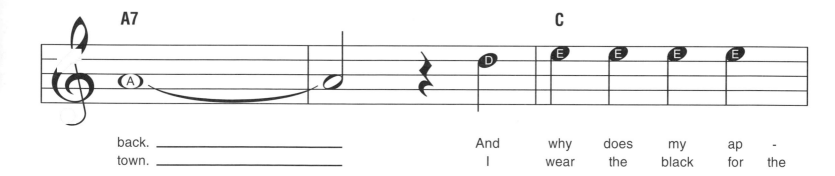

back. _____ And why does my ap -
town. _____ I wear the black for the

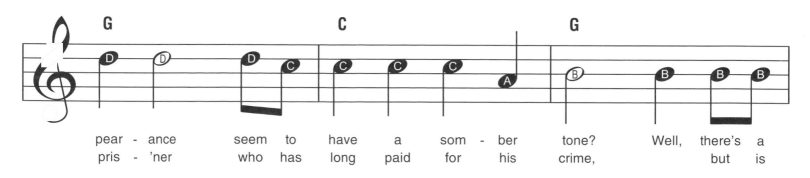

pear - ance seem to have a som - ber tone? Well, there's a
pris - 'ner who has long paid for his crime, but is

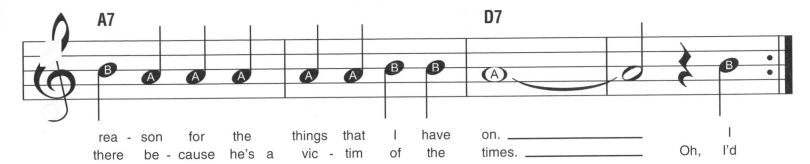

rea - son for the things that I have on. _____ I
there be - cause he's a vic - tim of the times. _____ Oh, I'd

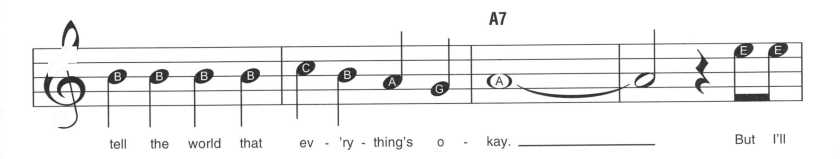

love to wear a rain - bow ev - 'ry day, _____ and

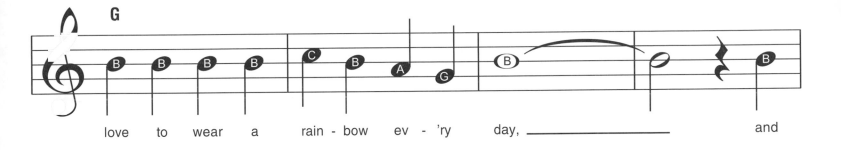

tell the world that ev - 'ry - thing's o - kay. _____ But I'll

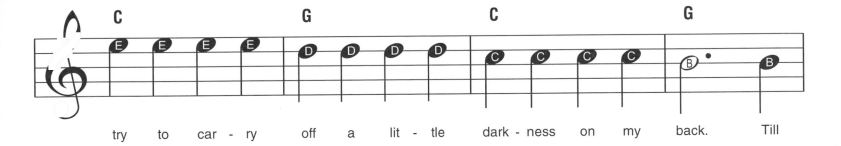

try to car - ry off a lit - tle dark - ness on my back. Till

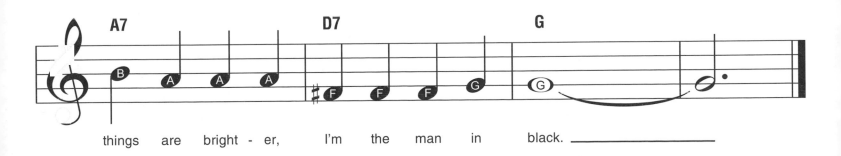

things are bright - er, I'm the man in black. _____

Ring of Fire

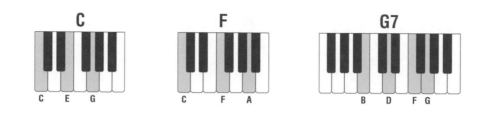

Words and Music by Merle Kilgore
and June Carter

Moderately fast

Love _____ is a burn - ing thing, _____ _____ and it makes _____ a fier - y ring. _____ Bound _____ _____ by wild de - sire, _____

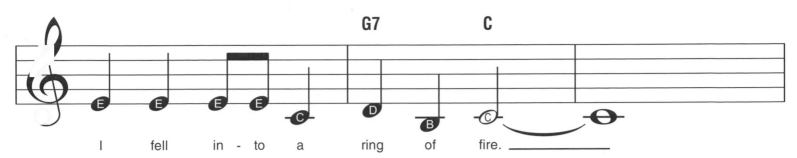

I fell in - to a ring of fire. _____

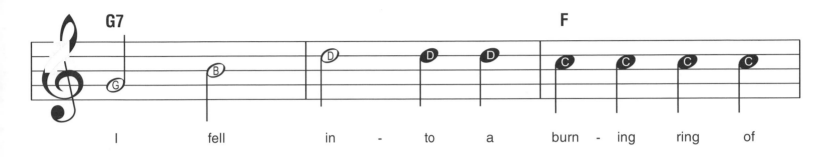

I fell in - to a burn - ing ring of

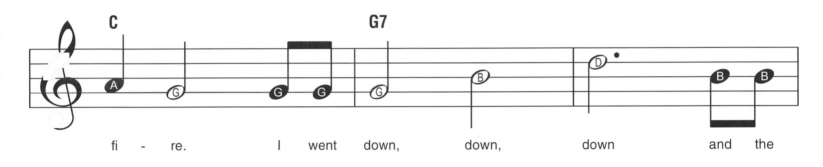

fi - re. I went down, down, down and the

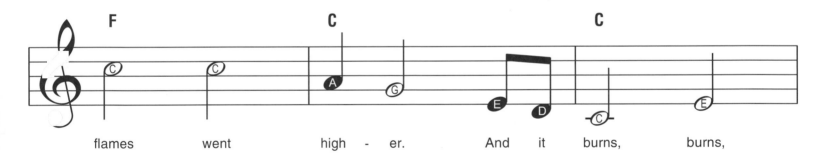

flames went high - er. And it burns, burns,

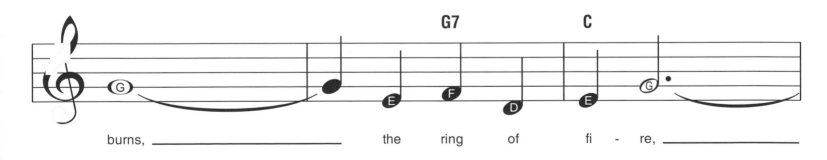

burns, _____ the ring of fi - re, _____

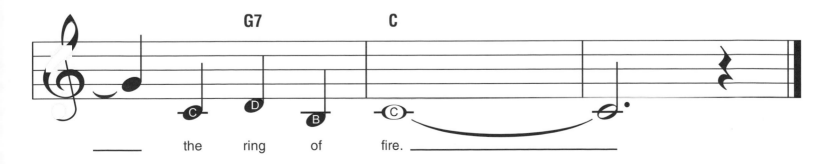

____ the ring of fire. _____

Sunday Mornin' Comin' Down

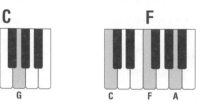
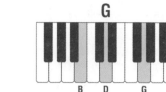

Words and Music by
Kris Kristofferson

On a Sun - day morn - in' side - walk,

I'm wish - in', Lord, that I was stoned.

'Cause there's some - thin' in a

Sun - day that makes a

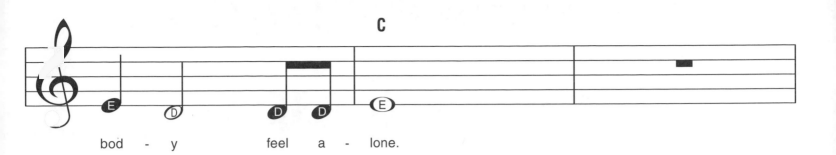

bod - y   feel   a - lone.

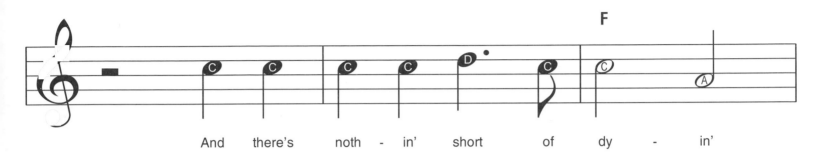

And   there's   noth - in'   short   of   dy - in'

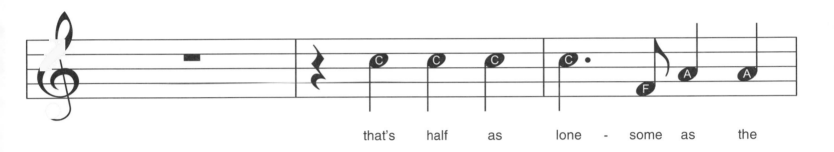

that's   half   as   lone - some   as   the

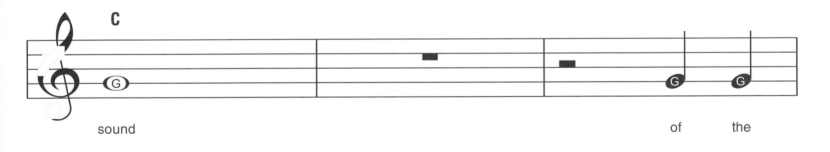

sound   of   the

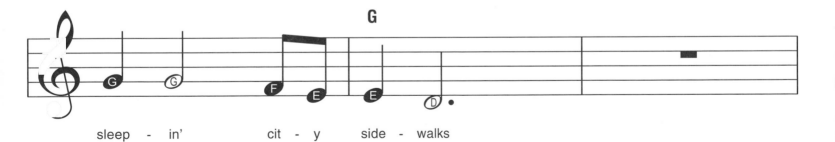

sleep - in'   cit - y   side - walks

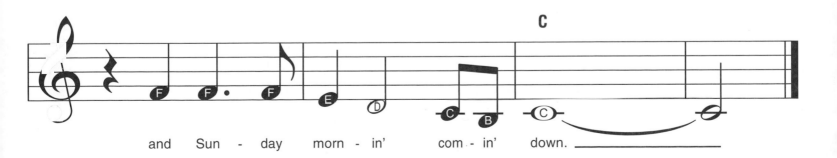

and   Sun - day   morn - in'   com - in'   down. _____

Tennessee Flat Top Box

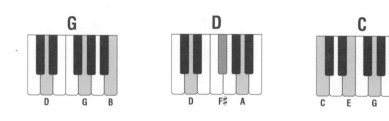

Words and Music by
John R. Cash

© 1961 (Renewed) UNICHAPPELL MUSIC, INC.
All Rights Reserved   Used by Permission

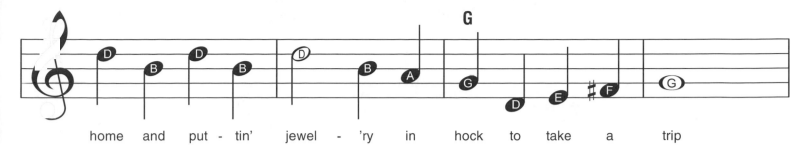

home and put - tin' jewel - 'ry in hock to take a trip

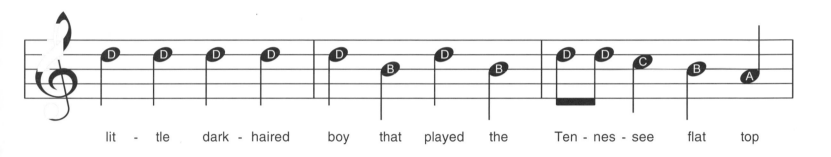

to go and lis - ten to the

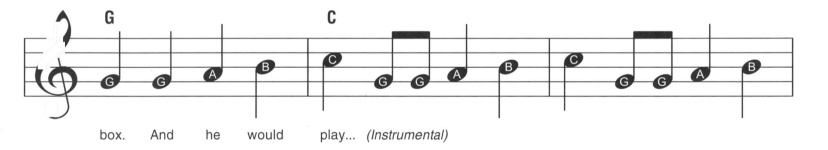

lit - tle dark - haired boy that played the Ten - nes - see flat top

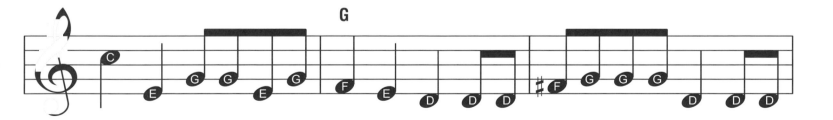

box. And he would play... *(Instrumental)*

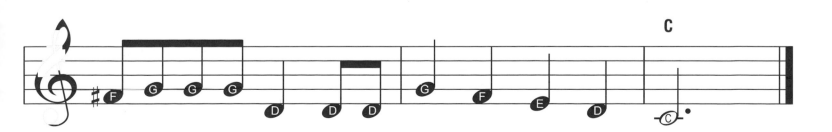

There You Go

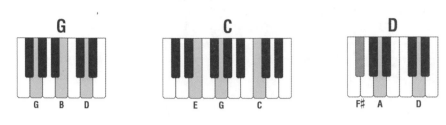

Words and Music by
Johnny Cash

Moderately bright

Well, here I am and there you go, you're gone a-gain. I know you're gon-na be the way you've al-ways been. Break-in' hearts and tell-in' lies is all you know. An-oth-er guy gives you the eye and

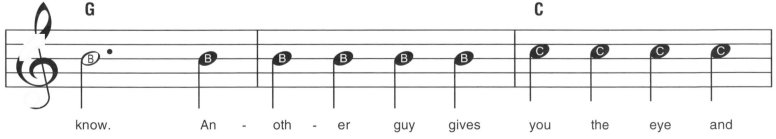

Understand Your Man

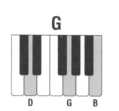
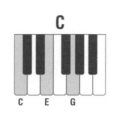
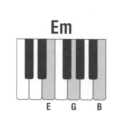
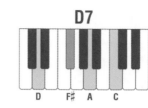
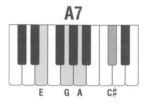

Words and Music by
John R. Cash

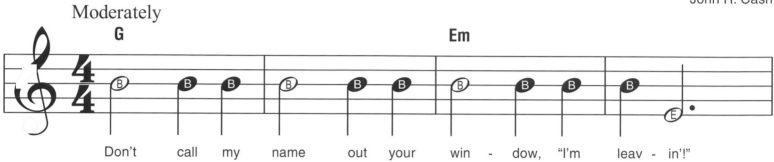

Don't call my name out your win - dow, "I'm leav - in'!"

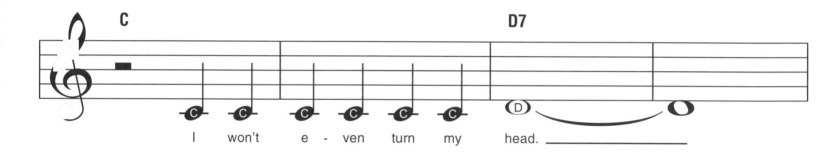

I won't e - ven turn my head. _____

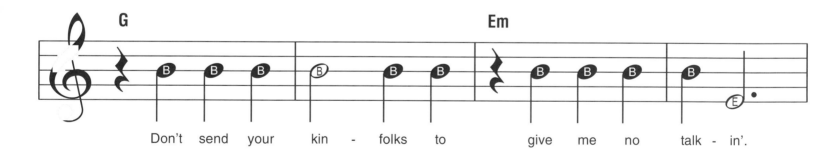

Don't send your kin - folks to give me no talk - in'.

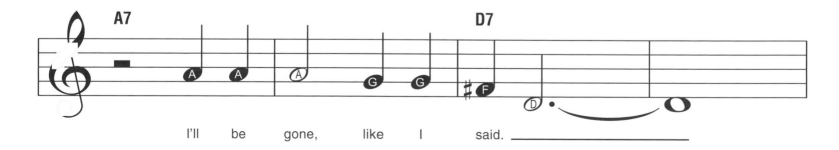

I'll be gone, like I said. _____

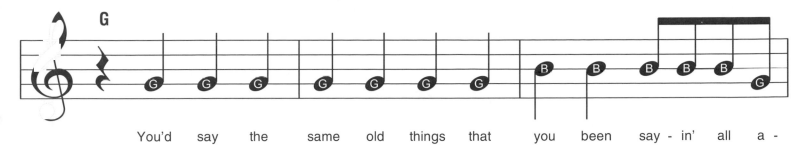

You'd say the same old things that you been say-in' all a-

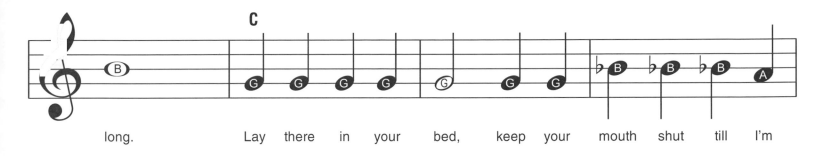

long. Lay there in your bed, keep your mouth shut till I'm

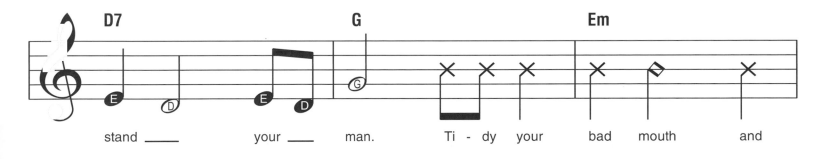

gone. _____ Don't give me that old fa - mil - iar

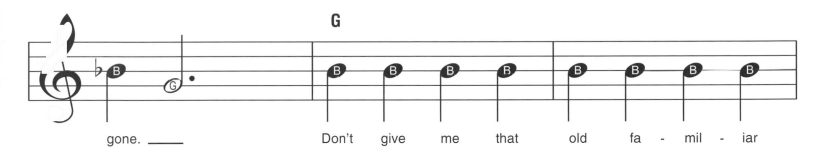

cry - in', cuss - in' moan. _____ Un - der -

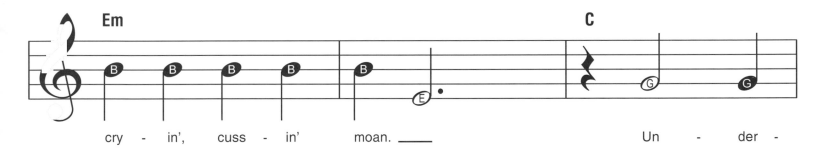

stand _____ your _____ man. Ti - dy your bad mouth and

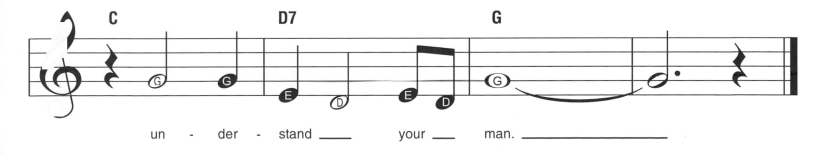

un - der - stand _____ your _____ man. _____

Jackson

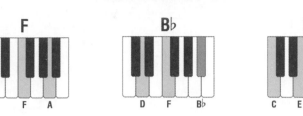

Words and Music by Billy Edd Wheeler
and Jerry Leiber

Moderately bright

We got mar-ried in a fe-ver, hot-ter than a pep-per sprout. We've been talk-in' 'bout Jack-son ev-er since the fire went out. I'm goin' to Jack-son. I'm gon-na mess a-round. Yeah, I'm goin' to Jack-son. Look out, Jack-son town.

INSTANT Piano Songs

Audio Access Included

The **Instant Piano Songs** series will help you play your favorite songs quickly and easily—whether you use one hand or two! Start with the melody in your right hand, adding basic left-hand chords when you're ready. Letter names inside each note speed up the learning process, and optional rhythm patterns take your playing to the next level. Online backing tracks are also included. Stream or download the tracks using the unique code inside each book, then play along to build confidence and sound great!

CLASSICAL THEMES

Air (from *Water Music*) (Handel) • Can Can (Offenbach) • Canon (Pachelbel) • Danube Waves (Ivanovici) • Funeral March of a Marionette (Gounod) • Für Elise (Beethoven) • Impromptu, Op. 142, No. 2 (Schubert) • Jesu, Joy of Man's Desiring (Bach) • Jupiter (Holst) • Lullaby (Brahms) • The Merry Widow Waltz (Lehár) • Minuet I (Bach) • The Moldau (Smetana) • Musette (Bach) • On the Beautiful Blue Danube (Strauss) • Over the Waves (Rosas) • Pomp and Circumstance (Elgar) • Prelude, Op. 28, No. 7 (Chopin) • Rondeau (Mouret) • St. Anthony Chorale (Haydn) • The Sleeping Beauty Waltz (Tchaikovsky) • Sonata K. 331 (Mozart) • Spring (Vivaldi) • Spring Song (Mendelssohn) • Symphony No. 9, Second Movement ("From the New World") (Dvořák) • Symphony No. 9, Fourth Movement ("Ode to Joy") (Beethoven) • To a Wild Rose (MacDowell) • Trumpet Tune (Purcell) • Trumpet Voluntary (Clarke) • William Tell Overture (Rossini).
00283826 Easy Piano Solo.. $14.99

DISNEY FAVORITES

The Ballad of Davy Crockett • The Bare Necessities • Beauty and the Beast • Bibbidi-Bobbidi-Boo (The Magic Song) • Can You Feel the Love Tonight • Chim Chim Cher-ee • Circle of Life • Colors of the Wind • A Dream Is a Wish Your Heart Makes • Evermore • Friend like Me • God Help the Outcasts • How Does a Moment Last Forever • How Far I'll Go • I See the Light • If I Never Knew You (End Title) • It's a Small World • Kiss the Girl • Lava • Let It Go • Let's Go Fly a Kite • Mickey Mouse March • Part of Your World • Reflection • Remember Me (Ernesto de la Cruz) • Supercalifragilisticexpialidocious • That's How You Know • When She Loved Me • A Whole New World • You'll Be in My Heart (Pop Version).
00283720 Easy Piano Solo...$14.99

MOVIE SONGS

Alfie • As Time Goes By • The Candy Man • City of Stars • Days of Wine and Roses • Endless Love • Hallelujah • I Will Always Love You • Laura • A Million Dreams • Mrs. Robinson • Moon River • My Heart Will Go on (Love Theme from 'Titanic') • Theme from "New York, New York" • Over the Rainbow • Raindrops Keep Fallin' on My Head • Secret Love • Singin' in the Rain • Skyfall • Somewhere, My Love • Somewhere Out There • Stayin' Alive • Take My Breath Away (Love Theme) • Tears in Heaven • The Trolley Song • Unchained Melody • Up Where We Belong • The Way We Were • What a Wonderful World • Where Do I Begin (Love Theme).
00283718 Easy Piano Solo..$14.99

POP HITS

All of Me • Can't Feel My Face • Chasing Cars • Despacito • Feel It Still • Happy • Havana • Hello • Hey, Soul Sister • Ho Hey • I Knew You Were Trouble • I'm Yours • Just Give Me a Reason • Let Her Go • Lost Boy • Love Yourself • Million Reasons • One Call Away • 100 Years • Perfect • Riptide • Say You Won't Let Go • See You Again • 7 Years • Shake It Off • Stay with Me • Thinking Out Loud • Viva La Vida • What Makes You Beautiful • You Are the Reason.
00283825 Easy Piano Solo..$14.99

HAL•LEONARD®

www.halleonard.com